50 STATES TO CELEBRATE

Celebrating
NEW JERSEY

www.hmhco.com

The text of this book is set in Weidemann.
The display type is set in Bernard Gothic.
The illustrations are drawn with pencil and colored digitally.
The maps are pen, ink, and watercolor.

Photograph of horses on page 32 © 2015 by Photodisc/Getty Images
Photograph of eastern goldfinch on page 32 © 2015 by William Leaman/Alamy
Photograph of common violet on page 32 © 2015 by Royal Freedman/Alamy

Library of Congress Cataloging-in-Publication Data
Kurtz, Jane.
Celebrating New Jersey / by Jane Kurtz ; illustrated by C. B. Canga.
p. cm.—(Greenlight readers) (50 states to celebrate)
Audience: Grades K–3.
ISBN 978-0-544-41977-3 paperback
ISBN 978-0-544-41978-0 paper over board
1. New Jersey—Juvenile literature. I. Canga, C. B., illustrator. II. Title.
F134.3.K88 2015
974.9—dc23
2014044084

Manufactured in China
SCP 10 9 8 7 6 5 4 3 2 1
4500532570

50 STATES TO CELEBRATE

Celebrating
NEW JERSEY

Written by **Jane Kurtz**
Illustrated by **C. B. Canga**

Green Light Readers

Houghton Mifflin Harcourt

Boston   New York

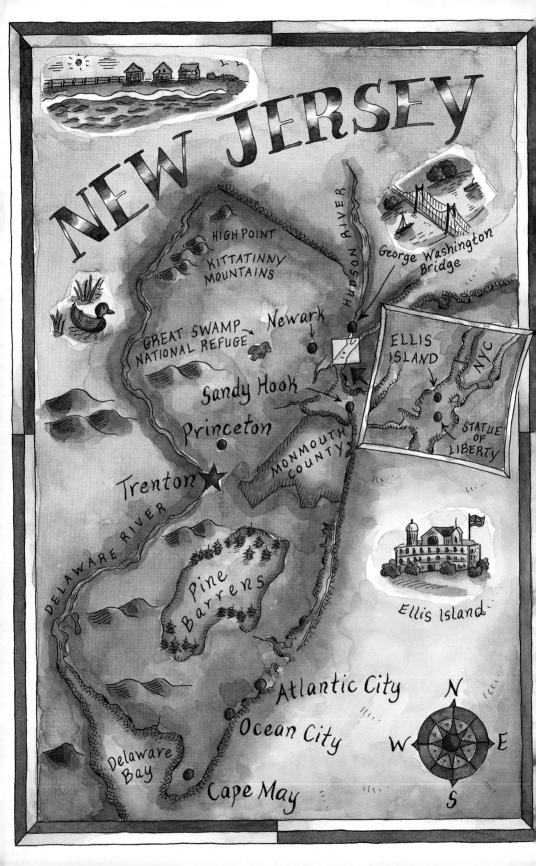

Hi, I'm Mr. Geo.

Welcome to New Jersey.

It has lots of people,

lots of cities,

lots of businesses,

and miles and miles of shoreline.

New Jersey is the fourth smallest state,
but it is the most **densely populated**.

1

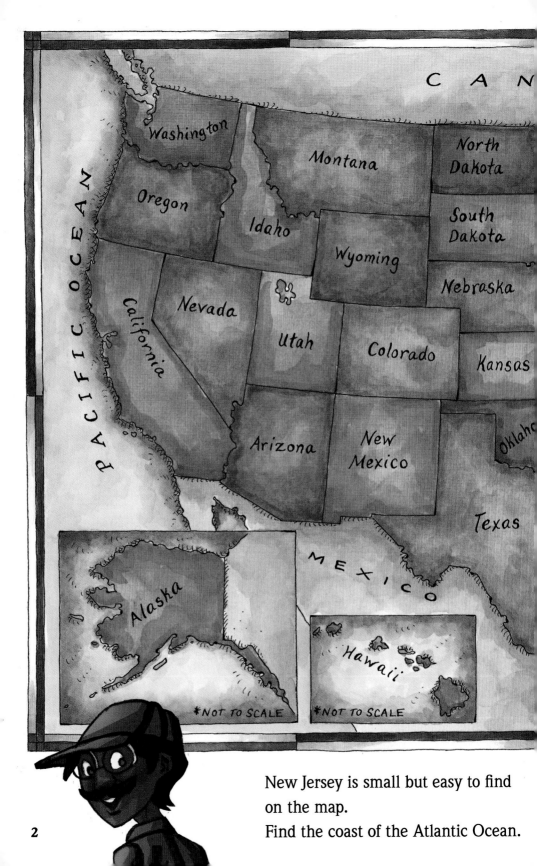

New Jersey is small but easy to find on the map.
Find the coast of the Atlantic Ocean.

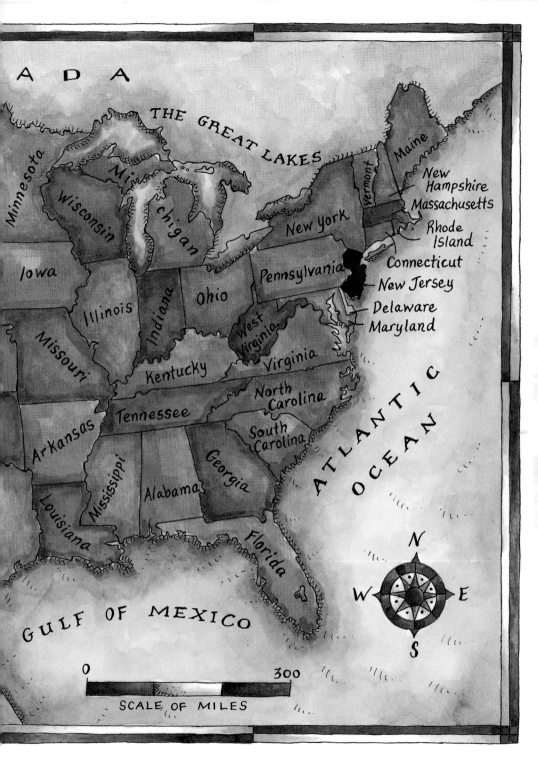

Now look south of New York,
and east of Pennsylvania.
Hello, New Jersey!

Let's start on the Jersey Shore.
This busy **boardwalk** in Ocean City
makes all my senses tingle.

I love the feel of the ocean breeze,
the smell of the salty air,
the whiz of the rides,
and the taste of saltwater taffy!

Many beaches on the Jersey Shore have boardwalks. The first boardwalk in the United States was built in Atlantic City, New Jersey, in 1870.

Now I'm in Cape May, to the south.
It's one of the oldest and prettiest
towns on the Jersey Shore.
Buildings look like gingerbread houses.
Beach pebbles sparkle like diamonds.
Seashells capture the sound of the sea.

My next stop along the coast?
Sandy Hook in northern New Jersey.
We can climb a 250-year-old lighthouse.
Wow! That's a great view of New York City.

Sandy Hook is home to the country's oldest
working lighthouse. It has kept ships in New
York Harbor safe since 1764.

I can't wait to see
the Statue of Liberty close up!
Liberty State Park in Jersey City
is just the place to start my trip.

MISS NEW JERSEY

Did you know? You can discover how **skyscrapers** are designed and built at the Liberty Science Center at Liberty State Park.

I can ride the ferry to Lady Liberty
and Ellis Island from here.
These **landmarks** welcomed millions of
immigrants to our country in the early 1900s.

Did you know?

Ellis Island is partly in New York but
mostly in New Jersey. It is home to the
Ellis Island Immigration Museum.

The Hudson River separates parts
of northern New Jersey from New York.
This historic tall ship
is taking us down the Hudson.

The *A.J. Meerwald* is New Jersey's official
tall ship. Its home port is Bivalve in
southern New Jersey, on Delaware Bay.

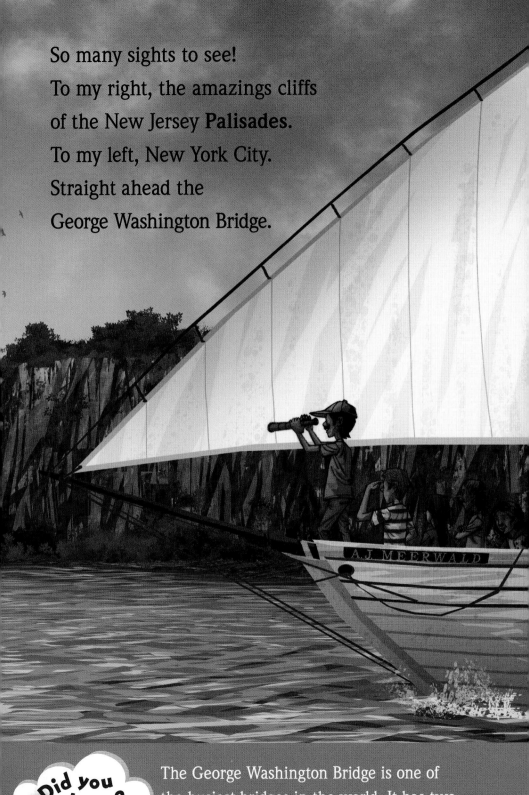

So many sights to see!
To my right, the amazings cliffs
of the New Jersey **Palisades**.
To my left, New York City.
Straight ahead the
George Washington Bridge.

A.J. MEERWALD

The George Washington Bridge is one of
the busiest bridges in the world. It has two
levels, 14 lanes, and a pedestrian walkway.

New Jersey has many places to escape traffic.
Here at High Point State Park,
I can camp, hike, swim, and SPLASH!

From the top of the Kittatinny Mountains in
High Point State Park, you can see three states—
New York, Pennsylvania, and New Jersey.

Mountains and forests surround me in this pretty **gorge** on the Delaware River. But all I want to do is float, spin, and stay right-side up!

Did you know?

The Delaware River forms the border between New Jersey and Pennsylvania.

13

New Jersey's first people were Native Americans.
The **Lenni Lenape** used canoes to fish
its rivers and streams.
They built **wigwams** and **longhouses**
to shelter their families.

Today, the Lenni Lenape share their traditions
and honor ancestors at **powwows.**
I love to see the colorful **regalia**
and lively dancing.

The names of many New Jersey towns come
from Native American words, including
Metuchen, Matawan, Passaic, and Secaucus.

New Jersey was one of the original 13 **colonies**.
Many important battles were fought here during
the **American Revolution**.

Some sites honor the night
George Washington and his soldiers
crossed the Delaware River.
Washington's daring plan led to victories
in Trenton and Princeton.

George Washington surprised the enemy by
crossing the dark and icy Delaware River on
Christmas night, December 25–26, 1776. **17**

I love watching **reenactments**.

Here I am at Monmouth Battlefield State Park.

That woman must be playing brave Molly Pitcher.

She brought water to wounded soldiers

during the American Revolution.

She took her husband's place on the battlefield.

Look! She's stuffing a **ramrod** into the cannon.

Boom! Boom! Boom!

Did you know?

Molly Pitcher got her nickname because she carried pitchers of water to thirsty soldiers. Her real name may have been Mary Ludwig Hays. 19

New Jersey has long been an industrial state.
In the 1800s, it was famous for making
locomotive trains and silk fabrics.
Zinc from this old mine helped produce
paint, tires, batteries, and brass instruments.

At the Sterling Hill Mine Museum you
can see **minerals** that glow in the dark!

Today, New Jersey companies make
hundreds of everyday products.
Shampoo and medicine.
Computer parts and home electronics.
Frozen foods and canned soups.
My favorite? Colorful candy-coated chocolates!

A famous American inventor
worked most of his life in New Jersey.
His name was Thomas Alva Edison.
His ideas for light bulbs, the **phonograph**,
and movie cameras changed the world.

This music room at Edison's lab is fun!
I'm listening to old-fashioned songs
on an antique phonograph.
Can you believe how big music players used to be?

Edison developed the first practical electric
light bulb at his lab in Menlo Park. Later, he
built a bigger lab in West Orange.

The southern part of New Jersey puts
the *garden* in the Garden State.
At Historic Cold Spring Village,
costumed guides show us country life from the past.
Hand me more veggies for the pepper pot soup!

Today, New Jersey has more than 10,000 farms.
Farmers grow more than 100 kinds
of fruits and vegetables.
Welcome to the Whitesbog Blueberry festival.
My tongue is still blue from the pie-eating contest!

New Jersey's main fruit crops are apples,
blueberries, cranberries, peaches, and
strawberries.

The Great Swamp National Wildlife Refuge
is a perfect place for bird-watching.
I saw Canada geese swimming,
eastern screech owls snoozing,
and red-tailed hawks hunting.

The Pine Barrens is also a nature **haven**.
It's full of marshes, **bogs**, and forests.
Want to join this sing-along by the campfire?
The treefrogs are singing with us!

The sandy soil of the Pine Barrens was once used to make glass and pottery.

New Jersey has many cities and big towns.

Trenton is the state capital.

Princeton has a world-famous university.

But I love this field in Secaucus.

Thirty robotic dinosaurs run and roar here!

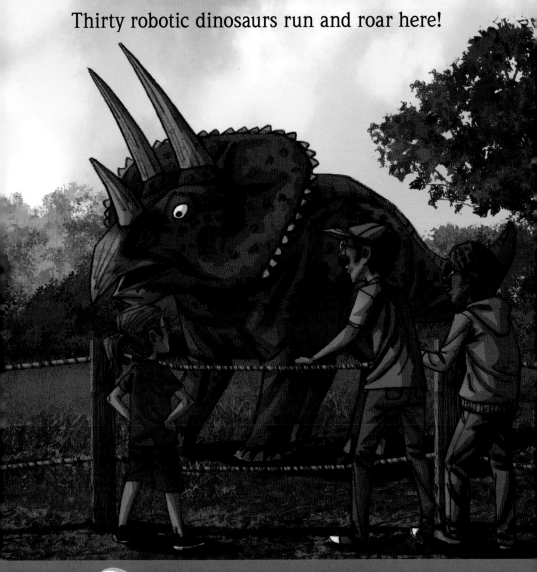

Paleontology, the study of dinosaurs, started with the discovery of a Hadrosaurus skeleton in Haddonfield, New Jersey, in 1858.

Newark is a big center for transportation.
Airplanes, ships, trains, and trucks
come and go all day.
The action at this music fest
in Lincoln Park is nonstop too.
Everyone has cool moves . . . even me!

The New Jersey Devils play hockey in Newark.
The New York Giants and New York Jets play
football in East Rutherford at the Meadowlands.

Wow! I've worked up an appetite.
Good thing this state is home to
so many all-night diners.

These disco fries are yummy!
Maybe I'll stick around for breakfast, too.
I'll never get my fill of New Jersey.

Fast Facts
About New Jersey

Nickname: The Garden State

State motto: Liberty and prosperity

State capital: Trenton

Other major cities: Newark, Jersey City, Elizabeth, Paterson, Clifton, Camden

Year of statehood: 1787

State mammal: Horse

State bird: Eastern goldfinch

State flower: The common violet

State flag:

Population: Approximately 8.9 million people, according to 2013 census.
Fun facts: The places named in the board game Monopoly are all real streets in Atlantic City, New Jersey.

Another fun fact: Many famous singers are from New Jersey, including Bruce Springsteen, Whitney Houston, Queen Latifah, the Jonas Brothers, Jon Bon Jovi, Frank Sinatra, and Frankie Valli.

Dates in New Jersey History

1200–1500: Three groups of Lenni Lenape live in the region.

1524: Giovanni de Verrazano explores the New Jersey area.

1609: Henry Hudson sails up the Hudson River, claims area for the Dutch.

1664: New Jersey becomes an English colony.

1776: General George Washington crosses the Delaware River from Pennsylvania into New Jersey for a surprise attack on the enemy during the American Revolution.

1777: Morristown serves as the winter headquarters for George Washington; serves as the headquarters again from 1779–80.

1778: The Battle of Monmouth.

1783: Princeton serves as the capital of the United States for several months during the end of the American Revolution.

1870: Atlantic City opens the first boardwalk.

1879: Thomas Edison demonstrates how the incandescent light bulb works to the public in Menlo Park.

1892: Ellis Island Immigration Station in New York Harbor opens.

1928: The Newark airport opens.

1931: The George Washington Bridge opens to traffic.

1998: The U.S. Supreme Court decides that Ellis Island is mainly in New Jersey.

2012: Hurricane Sandy causes major damage to many communities on the New Jersey shore.

Activities

1. **LOCATE** the three states that border New Jersey. Then, **SAY** each place's name out loud.

2. **DESIGN** a new license plate for New Jersey. Include a picture or short saying that tells something interesting about the state. Be creative, but leave room for the state name and license plate numbers. Write a sentence that explains why you created the design.

3. **SHARE** two facts you learned about New Jersey with a family member or friend.

4. **PRETEND** you are on a boardwalk in New Jersey and one of the arcades is having a game night. The game involves answering questions about New Jersey. If you win, you can play games at the arcade for free.

   a. **WHAT** is the name of the river that separates parts of northern New Jersey from New York?

   b. **WHAT** is the name of the river that separates New Jersey from Pennsylvania?

   c. **WHO** is the great inventor who worked most of his life in New Jersey?

   d. **WHERE** can you learn more about immigrants who came to this country in the early 1900s?

5. **UNJUMBLE** these words that have something to do with New Jersey. Write your answers on a separate sheet of paper.

   a. **TTRELSWAA YATFF** (HINT: a chewy candy)

   b. **WKAORALBD** (HINT: It's made of wood)

c. **RLBBEEEURIS** (HINT: a fruit grown in New Jersey)

d. **APHHORGPNO** (HINT: one of Thomas Edison's inventions)

FOR ANSWERS, SEE PAGE 36.

Glossary

American Revolution: the war that won the 13 American colonies freedom from British rule; it took place from 1775 to 1783. (p. 16)

boardwalk: a public walkway that is located along a beach and made of wooden planks. (p. 4)

bog: an area of wet, spongy ground. (p. 27)

colony: a settlement ruled by another country. (p. 16)

densely populated: having a large number of people in relation to the amount of space of an area; for example, a big city is more densely populated than a small town. (p. 1)

disco fries: cheese fries with gravy. (p. 31)

gorge: a deep, narrow valley with very steep sides; a stream or river often runs through a gorge. (p. 13)

haven: a safe place. (p. 27)

immigrants: people who move to a country from another country. (p. 9)

landmark: a familiar or easily seen object or building that identifies a place; for example, the Statue of Liberty is a landmark of New York City and northern New Jersey. (p. 9)

Lenni Lenape: a Native American people who lived along the Delaware River; also called the Delaware. (p. 14)

longhouse: a type of Native American dwelling designed to house several families. (p. 14)

mineral: a natural, nonliving substance that is mined for human use; examples of minerals include gold, silver, coal, iron ore, rock, and zinc. (p. 20)

palisades: a line of high cliffs, usually upon a river. (p. 11)

phonograph: a machine that reproduces sound, usually music, from a flat disk called a record. (p. 22)

powwow: a Native American ceremony that often involves singing, dancing, and feasting. (p. 15)

ramrod: a rod used to force the charge in a cannon to fire. (p. 19)

reenactment: an occasion on which people reenact an event; the event is often of historical importance. (p. 18)

regalia: traditional outfits used in Native American ceremonies and celebrations, including powwows; regalia is an expression of spirit and has often been prayed over and blessed. (p. 15)

skyscraper: a tall building. (p. 8)

wigwam: a type of Native American dwelling made of poles that are bent to form a dome and covered with bark or animal hides. (p. 14)

Answers to Activities on page 34:

1) Pennsylvania, New York, and Delaware; 2) Drawings will vary; 3) Answers will vary; 4a) Hudson River, 4b) Delaware River, 4c) Thomas Alva Edison, 4d) Ellis Island Immigration Museum and/or the Statue of Liberty; 5a) saltwater taffy, 5b) boardwalk, 5c) blueberries, 5d) phonograph.